I0793512

The INSIDE GUIDE

DOCUMENTS OF DEMOCRACY

Common Sense

By Sadie Silva

Cavendish Square
New York

Published in 2022 by Cavendish Square Publishing, LLC
29 East 21st Street, New York, NY 10010

First Edition

Website: cavendishsq.com

Portions of this work were originally authored by Ryan Nagelhout and published as *Thomas Paine's* Common Sense *(Documents That Shaped America).* All new material this edition authored by Sadie Silva.

Library of Congress Cataloging-in-Publication Data

Names: Silva, Sadie, author.
Title: Common sense / Sadie Silva.
Description: New York : Cavendish Square Publishing, 2022. | Series: The inside guide. Documents of democracy | Includes index.
Identifiers: LCCN 2020046271 | ISBN 9781502660480 (library binding) | ISBN 9781502660466 (paperback) | ISBN 9781502660473 (set) | ISBN 9781502660497 (ebook)
Subjects: LCSH: Paine, Thomas, 1737-1809. Common sense–Juvenile literature. | Paine, Thomas, 1737-1809–Juvenile literature. | United States–Politics and government–1775-1783–Juvenile literature. | Political science–History–18th century–Juvenile literature.
Classification: LCC E211.P153 S55 2022 | DDC 320.51092 [B]–dc23
LC record available at https://lccn.loc.gov/2020046271

Editor: Caitie McAneney
Copyeditor: Jill Keppeler
Designer: Jessica Nevins

The photographs in this book are used by permission and through the courtesy of: Cover courtesy of Library of Congress; pp. 4, 29 (top) Bettmann/Getty Images; pp. 6, 27 (bottom) Joe Sohm/Visions of America/Universal Images Group via Getty Images; pp. 7, 10 Courtesy of the Library of Congress Rare Book and Special Collections Division; p. 8 Universal History Archive/Getty Images; p. 9 Fotosearch/Getty Images; p. 12 ullstein bild/ullstein bild via Getty Images; pp. 13, 18, 20 Hulton Archive/Getty Images; pp. 14, 25 (top) The Print Collector/Print Collector/Getty Images; p. 15 Apic/Getty Images; p. 16 Heritage Art/Heritage Images via Getty Images; pp. 21 (top), 22, 24, 26, 27 (top) Courtesy of the Library of Congress Prints and Photographs Division; p. 21 (bottom) Francis Miller/The LIFE Picture Collection via Getty Images; p. 25 (bottom) Lee Snider/The Image Bank Unreleased/Getty Images; p. 29 (bottom) Stock Montage/Stock Montage/Getty Images.

CPSIA compliance information: Batch #CW22CSQ: For further information contact Cavendish Square Publishing LLC, New York, New York, at 1-877-980-4450.

Printed in the United States of America

CONTENTS

Thomas Paine was known for his bold ideas and plain-spoken arguments for democracy.

THE BACKDROP OF REVOLUTION

Chapter One

When Thomas Paine wrote his famous pamphlet at the onset of the American Revolution, he hoped to offer "simple facts, plain arguments, and common sense." Published on January 10, 1776, the pamphlet sent shock waves throughout Britain's American colonies, leading many colonists to favor revolution. *Common Sense* became one of the most important documents of the American Revolution, a call to action for colonists to rebel against England and fight for **democracy**.

Coming to America

Thomas Paine was born in 1737. He worked different jobs in England, but he developed a talent for writing about injustice. He was fired as a tax collector, or excise officer, after writing a pamphlet demanding better pay for excise officers. He'd printed 4,000 copies and gave them out, even to members of the British **Parliament**.

Paine met Benjamin Franklin in London, England, in 1774. Franklin would become one of the key **Founding Fathers** of the United States. Impressed by Paine, Franklin encouraged him to make the long voyage to the American colonies. Paine arrived on November 30, 1774. He became the first editor of the *Pennsylvania Magazine* in Philadelphia, Pennsylvania.

THOMAS PAINE

Thomas Paine was born in Thetford, England, on January 29, 1737. Paine's father was a **Quaker** and stay maker. Many stay makers made **corsets**, but those in the shipbuilding center of Thetford likely sewed ship sails. Paine left school when he was 12 to work alongside his father. Thomas Paine was 37 when he traveled to America from England. Soon after, he wrote *Common Sense* and other works. By the time he died in 1809, at 72 years old, much of the young nation had forgotten him. His writing, however, stood the test of time and influenced many American documents of democracy.

Fast Fact

Many biographies of Paine call him a corset maker. The Thomas Paine National Historical Association says the rumor of his corset making was spread to make him seem less of a hero.

This model shows Thomas Paine at work in his home in New Rochelle, New York.

THE
PENNSYLVANIA
MAGAZINE:
OR,
AMERICAN
MONTHLY MUSEUM.
MDCCLXXV.
VOLUME I.

Benjamin Franklin helped Thomas Paine land a job as the first editor of the *Pennsylvania Magazine*.

He'd come to America on the eve of the revolution, as tension was high and change was in the air.

Unrest in the Colonies

For much of the American colonies' existence, there had been good relations with Britain. The French and Indian War (1754–1763) changed things. Britain spent a lot of money protecting its North American lands from France during this conflict, so it then decided to enforce taxes on the colonists. The slogan "Taxation without representation is **tyranny**" later became a rallying cry.

When Paine wrote *Common Sense*, the fighting of the American Revolution had already begun.

Fast Fact

Paine's *Common Sense* was published a few months after Britain's King George III made a speech to Parliament stating the colonies were in open rebellion against the crown.

The Boston Tea Party on December 16, 1773, was a colonial protest over the British tax on tea.

There had been battles at Lexington and Concord in Massachusetts in April 1775, and American troops had moved into British-controlled Canada. However, there was no official declaration of war. Many people still needed to be persuaded toward independence—and *Common Sense* filled that need.

An Englishman Appeals to Americans

Common Sense was the first written work to openly called for American independence. The pamphlet was first published anonymously, or without Paine's name on it. The pamphlet said it was "Written by an Englishman." Paine, like other colonists, still considered himself to be British. Many **grievances** in *Common Sense* describe wrongdoings in England. Having lived in England his entire life, Paine had more knowledge about that country than about the colonies. Even though he was an outsider, Paine's

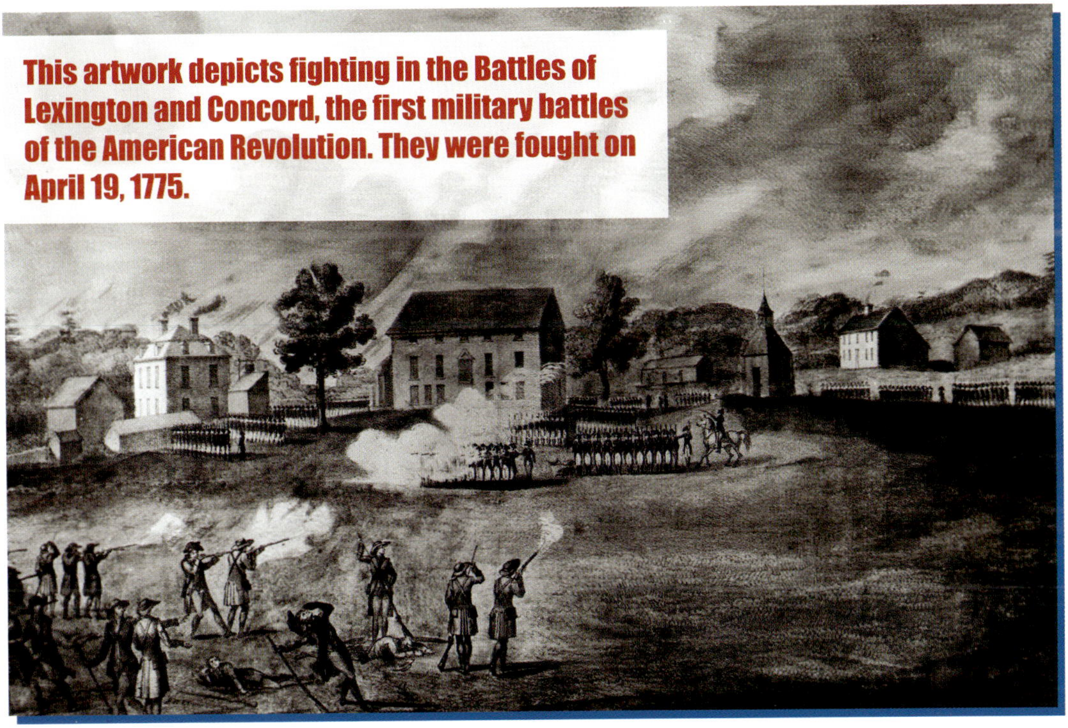

This artwork depicts fighting in the Battles of Lexington and Concord, the first military battles of the American Revolution. They were fought on April 19, 1775.

Common Sense convinced many weary and uncertain colonists that separation from England was the only option. The short pamphlet was bought—and read—in huge numbers. It sold 120,000 copies in just the first three months.

Part of what made *Common Sense* so successful was that it was easy for colonists to understand, even those without much education. Paine wrote in plain terms about important ideas from thinkers throughout history. In fact, Thomas Paine almost gave *Common Sense* the title *Plain Truth*. The practical language of *Common Sense* appealed to the common people.

Fast Fact

Some colonists, called Loyalists, were loyal to King George III, while others, the patriots, wanted to break from England.

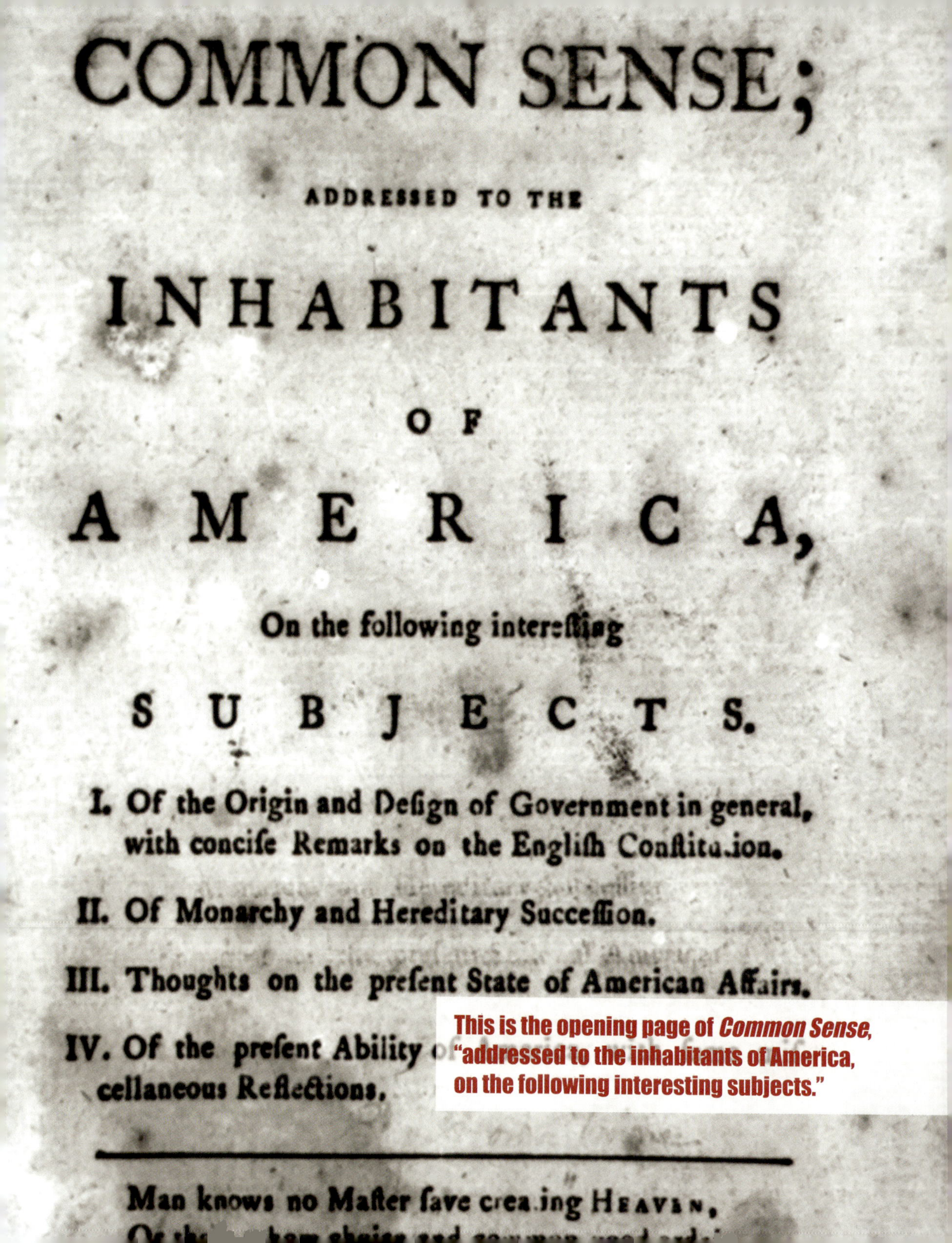

COMMON SENSE;

ADDRESSED TO THE

INHABITANTS

OF

AMERICA,

On the following intereſting

SUBJECTS.

I. Of the Origin and Deſign of Government in general, with conciſe Remarks on the Engliſh Conſtitution.

II. Of Monarchy and Hereditary Succeſſion.

III. Thoughts on the preſent State of American Affairs.

IV. Of the preſent Ability o
cellaneous Reflections.

Man knows no Maſter ſave creating HEAVEN,

This is the opening page of *Common Sense*, "addressed to the inhabitants of America, on the following interesting subjects."

GOVERNMENT AND GRIEVANCES

Chapter Two

In the introduction to *Common Sense*, Thomas Paine states that he's aware the ideas in his pamphlet may not be widely accepted by the public. However, he writes, "Time makes more **converts** than reason." He knew a call for independence may not be popular, but that it was right.

Common Sense is arranged in four main parts. The first two parts focus on the origins and functions of government and grievances with the monarchy, or king-led government, of England.

The Origins of Government

The first part of *Common Sense* is entitled "Of the Origin and Design of Government in General, with Concise Remarks on the English Constitution." In the pamphlet's opening pages, Paine points out the differences between society and government. Society, he argues, exists because it's easier for people to live together than alone. A government should exist only to protect society from the evils of people. A monarchy, according to Paine, doesn't fulfill the needs of the people. A proper government is elected by the people.

Much *of Common Sense* argues against the need for a king or queen. Paine makes a case against a constitutional monarchy—a type of

John Locke (1632–1704) was a British philosopher, or thinker, who inspired Thomas Paine's ideas on citizens' rights and the function of government.

government in which Parliament makes laws and a king or queen enforces them. He felt this kind of government didn't limit the monarch's power enough. To Paine, the common people would be better off without a monarch and with only an elected government. Paine also argued that the English were only in favor of their king because of national pride, not reason.

England's Wrongdoings

The second section of *Common Sense* is called "Of Monarchy and Heredity." In it, Paine argued that it's wrong to divide mankind into kings and subjects. He wrote that "exalting one man so greatly above the rest cannot be justified on the equal rights of nature." He even used examples from the Bible to support his idea that a monarchy isn't just unfair—it's a sin.

BIG IDEAS

Thomas Paine was influenced by the ideas of **Enlightenment** thinkers, Bible passages, and the Magna Carta. Enlightenment thinker John Locke believed all men had natural rights, including the rights to life, liberty, and property. Locke also described a "social contract" people agree to when they create a government, thoughts echoed by Paine in *Common Sense*. Paine's Quaker upbringing gave him a good knowledge of the Bible, and he used it to appeal to the Christian colonists. Paine's religious references stress that all men are created equal, which he thought rejected the very idea of kings. Paine later references the Magna Carta, which introduced elements of democracy to England in 1215.

This 1719 illustration shows a meeting of Quakers.

Fast Fact

The Society of Friends, also known as Quakers, is a Christian group first established in 17th-century England. It opposes war and rejects certain Christian traditions, such as having official ministers.

This artwork shows King John signing the Magna Carta, which Paine references in his work.

This section discusses the "tyranny" of the British government, finding fault with the monarchy and the upper class. Paine argued that the common people should be represented in government, not lorded over by the rich and powerful. He also discussed the **hereditary** nature of the crown, arguing that it adds to the "evil of monarchy." Paine wrote, "… such an unwise, unjust, unnatural compact might (perhaps) in the next **succession** put them under the government of a rogue or a fool." According to Paine, by allowing hereditary rule, Britain was open to foolish, wicked rulers, as well as some too young to lead effectively.

Fast Fact

In 1215, King John of England was pressured to sign the Magna Carta, or "Great Charter," which gave barons certain rights while limiting the power of the king.

Paine further argued that monarchies make their subjects fight violent wars on their behalf, while a representative government would fight only wars believed necessary by the people. Paine wrote, "In short, monarchy and succession have laid (not this or that kingdom only) but the world in blood and ashes." Paine's words against the monarchy were a harsh criticism of British rule.

Fast Fact

Thomas Paine wrote, "Of more worth is one honest man to society and in the sight of God, than all the crowned ruffians that ever lived."

King George III (1738–1820) ruled England for nearly 60 years and was seen by many colonists as a tyrant.

Thomas Paine called for the American colonists to take action to become an independent nation, which happened through revolution. George Washington, shown here shaking the hand of the Marquis de Lafayette (an important French ally during the war), led the fight for independence.

A CALL TO ACTION

Chapter Three

The first two sections of *Common Sense* made a clear case for why American colonists shouldn't live under British rule. The next two sections were a call to action. They urged colonists to declare independence, use their strengths, and form a just government for the people by the people.

Independence and a New Start

Paine titled the third section "Thoughts on the Present State of American Affairs." In this section, Paine laid out only one choice for the colonists: fight for independence. He wrote, "Arms, as the last resource, decide the contest; the appeal was the choice of the king, and the continent hath accepted the challenge." This means that fighting a revolution was the only answer since the king would not make amends.

> **Fast Fact**
>
> Paine spoke against the argument that colonists should stay loyal because England had defended them in the past. Paine noted there were important differences between the interests of the colonies and the interests of England when it came to defense.

Common Sense also stressed that the colonies needed to unite under common goals, though their desires were varied.

THE ECONOMIC POTENTIAL OF AMERICA

Paine believed in the colonies' ability to go it alone—and argued that they'd actually be better off economically. One of the most striking statements made in *Common Sense* is that the colonies would prosper without British involvement in America's economy. "America would have flourished as much, and probably much more, had no European power taken any notice of her," Paine wrote. He stated that the products made in the colonies could be sold to anyone and suggested they were held back by British trade limits and taxes. Since the creation of the colonies, they could only trade with England, which limited their economic potential.

Britain practiced mercantilism, a system in which its colonies couldn't make certain goods and could only trade with England. England also enforced harsh taxes on certain products, which the colonists protested, as shown here.

They needed an official declaration of their intention to self-govern. Paine saw unity as the only path to success.

Fast Fact

Paine didn't support the two-house Congress with a larger House of Representatives and a smaller Senate. He also thought the Constitution should be rewritten at the will of the people.

Paine wrote an outline for a new governing body for the "United Colonies," suggesting that each colony should send at least 30 delegates to this congress, which would meet each year and elect a president, not a king. A colony would be chosen at random each year, and a president would be picked from that colony. The congress was also charged with making laws. Three-fifths of the representatives would need to support a law in order for it to pass.

Though the Founding Fathers did end up creating a congress, it looked different from Paine's idea. The government set up by the U.S. Constitution has three branches—executive, legislative, and judicial. Congress, the legislative branch, has two houses called the Senate and House of Representatives. The president, who heads the executive branch, is elected indirectly by the people.

Fast Fact

Paine's plan called for representatives from each colony to come together to write a "Continental Charter," an outline of a new governing body like the Magna Carta. The colonies would work together to form an agreement.

As Paine suggested, the Founding Fathers did craft their own constitution. In 1787, George Washington presided over, or led, what's now called the Constitutional Convention.

The Strengths of the Colonies

The final section of *Common Sense* is entitled "Of the Present Ability of America, with Some Miscellaneous Reflexions." This section discusses the potential of the American colonies to not only fight but win a war for independence. Listing the continent's natural resources—like iron and gunpowder—Paine describes in detail the costs to build a navy that could compete with the powerful British naval forces.

Fast Fact

Paine wrote that it was wiser and safer to make a constitution together in a "cool deliberate manner" than to leave it to chance.

Thomas Paine wrote, "No country on the globe is so happily situated, or so internally capable of raising a [naval] fleet as America."

Paine was confident this war was one the colonists could win. He concluded *Common Sense* by telling his audience that though it may feel "strange and difficult" to declare independence, it will become familiar and agreeable in time. He wrote that independence was necessary.

Fast Fact

Soon after publishing *Common Sense*, Paine joined the army and helped fight for the cause he had so convincingly supported in his writings. It's said that he even donated his earnings from *Common Sense* to the Continental Army.

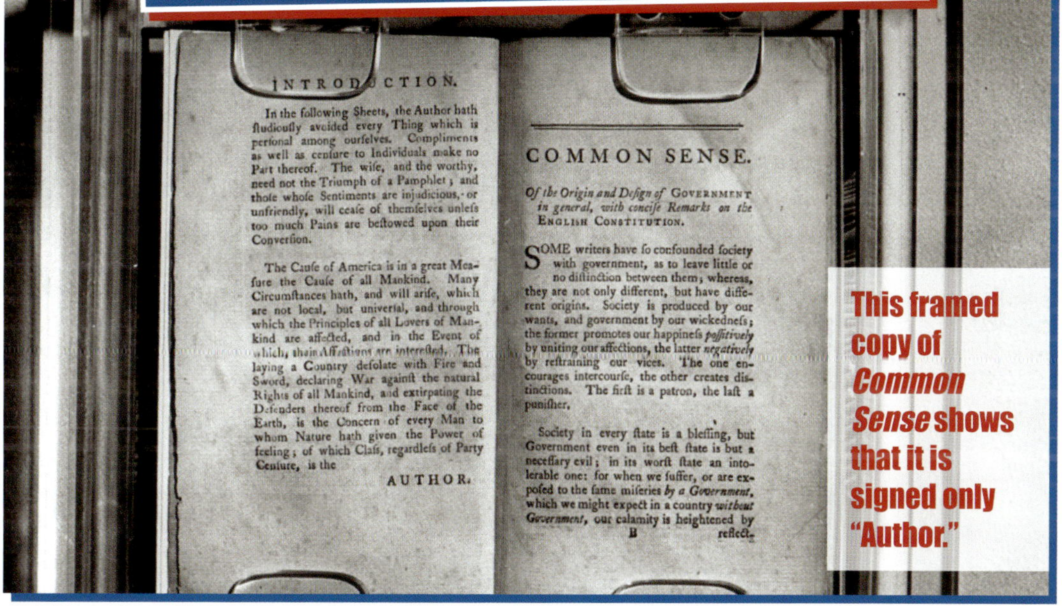

INTRODUCTION.

In the following Sheets, the Author hath ſtudiouſly avoided every Thing which is perſonal among ourſelves. Compliments as well as cenſure to Individuals make no Part thereof. The wiſe, and the worthy, need not the Triumph of a Pamphlet; and thoſe whoſe Sentiments are injudicious, or unfriendly, will ceaſe of themſelves unleſs too much Pains are beſtowed upon their Converſion.

The Cauſe of America is in a great Meaſure the Cauſe of all Mankind. Many Circumſtances hath, and will ariſe, which are not local, but univerſal, and through which the Principles of all Lovers of Mankind are affected, and in the Event of which, their Affections are intereſted. The laying a Country deſolate with Fire and Sword, declaring War againſt the natural Rights of all Mankind, and extirpating the Defenders thereof from the Face of the Earth, is the Concern of every Man to whom Nature hath given the Power of feeling; of which Claſs, regardleſs of Party Cenſure, is the

AUTHOR.

COMMON SENSE.

Of the Origin and Deſign of GOVERNMENT *in general, with conciſe Remarks on the* ENGLISH CONSTITUTION.

SOME writers have ſo confounded ſociety with government, as to leave little or no diſtinction between them; whereas, they are not only different, but have different origins. Society is produced by our wants, and government by our wickedneſs; the former promotes our happineſs *poſitively* by uniting our affections, the latter *negatively* by reſtraining our vices. The one encourages intercourſe, the other creates diſtinctions. The firſt is a patron, the laſt a puniſher.

Society in every ſtate is a bleſſing, but Government even in its beſt ſtate is but a neceſſary evil; in its worſt ſtate an intolerable one: for when we ſuffer, or are expoſed to the ſame miſeries *by a Government*, which we might expect in a country *without Government*, our calamity is heightened by

B reflect-

This framed copy of *Common Sense* shows that it is signed only "Author."

This artwork shows (from right to left) Thomas Jefferson, John Adams, and Benjamin Franklin reviewing a draft of the Declaration of Independence.

INFLUENTIAL IDEAS

Chapter Four

Thomas Paine's ideas about independence, equality, and revolution were **radical**. They weren't popular with everyone, and Paine had his share of critics. However, his ideas helped spark a movement toward independence—and toward the founding of the United States.

Uniting for Independence

In early 1776, colonists were still divided on the issue of independence, even as the unrest became more violent. However, after the publication of *Common Sense*, many colonists rallied around Paine's pamphlet, crying for unity.

Paine even influenced local governments to write declarations of independence using language from *Common Sense*. Just a few months after *Common Sense* was published, Thomas Jefferson penned the official Declaration of Independence on behalf of all the colonies. Jefferson borrowed language and ideas from Enlightenment thinkers as well as Paine. The Declaration of Independence shares Paine's ideas of equality among men, grievances with the king, and the path to independence.

Fast Fact

The Declaration of Independence was adopted by the Second Continental Congress on July 4, 1776.

President Theodore Roosevelt (1858–1919) disliked Paine's *The Age of Reason* because it criticized Christianity.

Common Sense Critics

Common Sense wasn't published under Thomas Paine's name right away. Still, he faced criticism for his big, sometimes **unconventional** ideas. Founding Father John Adams described Paine as a man able to tear a house down but lacking the skills to rebuild it.

Some called Paine out for his remarks against organized religion. President Theodore Roosevelt once called Paine "a dirty little atheist." However, an atheist is a person who doesn't believe in God, and Paine did believe in God. Many misrepresentations of Paine have been passed down by his critics.

Even after the colonists had gained independence, Paine **advocated** for sharing wealth with the poor, ending slavery, and expanding women's rights. These ideas were unfamiliar and even shocking at the time.

Common Sense made a bold argument against the traditional European social order of the 1700s, which interested French

Fast Fact

Later in life, Paine had a falling out with the Quakers and was refused burial in a Quaker cemetery when he died.

John Adams (1735–1826) wrote in his autobiography about his dislike of Thomas Paine, calling Paine a "Star of Disaster."

revolutionaries in the years after the American Revolution. Paine even went to France to help with the French Revolution from 1792 to 1795, but he was imprisoned by the revolutionaries when he didn't agree with the bloody execution, or killing, of King Louis XVI.

Paine's Legacy

Thomas Paine's influence lives on in his writings. At one point, *Common Sense* was one of the most-read works in the Western world. During the American Revolution, he wrote another influential pamphlet called *The Crisis* (also known as *The American Crisis*). During the 1790s, *The Rights of Man* was published in two parts, as well as

Among his many famous words, Paine's essays in *The Crisis* were some of the first works to use the term "United States of America."

THE CRISIS

Paine's series of 16 pamphlets entitled *The Crisis* (also called *The American Crisis*) was published at a difficult point in the American Revolution. The first pamphlet, published on December 23, 1776, begins with the now-famous line: "These are the times that try men's souls." Paine wrote it as the colonies struggled to fight against the British forces. *The Crisis* helped rally the new Americans against the British troops. General George Washington thought the first *Crisis* essay was so inspiring that he ordered it read aloud to troops at Valley Forge, Pennsylvania, during the deadly winter of 1776–1777. Paine's words inspired bravery, purpose, and hope.

The first winter of the American Revolution proved deadly for American troops at Valley Forge. This artwork shows George Washington praying there.

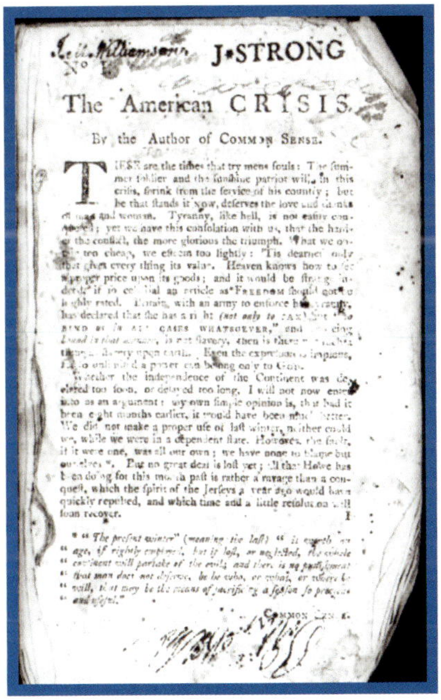

J•STRONG

The American CRISIS.

By the Author of COMMON SENSE.

In Thomas Paine's moving work *The Crisis*, he wrote, "The harder the conflict, the more glorious the triumph."

the first two parts of *The Age of Reason*. Both offered support for the French Revolution.

In 1802, Paine returned to America and lived the rest of his life on his farm in New Rochelle, New York. He died on June 8, 1809. Just about a dozen people attended his funeral. His bones were later dug up for a proper reburial but then lost.

Fast Fact

Thomas Jefferson said of Thomas Paine, "No writer has exceeded Paine in ease and familiarity of style ... and in simple and unassuming language."

Paine may not have always been popular with everyone, but over time, his legacy grew. *Common Sense* helped to shape the democratic ideals of the United States of America, sparking a worldwide movement toward freedom, equality, and democracy for all.

Thomas Paine's burial site is in New Rochelle, New York.

REVOLUTIONARY QUOTES FROM *COMMON SENSE*

Part I:

- "Society in every state is a blessing, but government even in its best state is but a necessary evil; in its worst state an intolerable one."
- "There is something exceedingly ridiculous in the composition of monarchy."
- "The prejudice of Englishmen, in favour of their own government by king, lords and commons, arises as much or more from national pride than reason."

Part II:

- "As the exalting one man so greatly above the rest cannot be justified on the equal rights of nature, so neither can it be defended on the authority of scripture."
- "But it is not so much the absurdity as the evil of hereditary succession which concerns mankind. Did it ensure a race of good and wise men it would have the seal of divine authority, but as it opens a door to the foolish, the wicked, and the improper, it hath in it the nature of oppression."
- "In short, monarchy and succession have laid (not this or that kingdom only) but the world in blood and ashes."

Part III:

- "Now is the seed time of continental union, faith and honor."
- "But Britain is the parent country, say some. Then the more shame upon her conduct."
- "A government of our own is our natural right."
- "O ye that love mankind! Ye that dare oppose, not only the tyranny, but the tyrant, stand forth!"

Part IV:

- "It is not in numbers, but in unity, that our great strength lies."
- "No country on the globe is so happily situated, or so internally capable of raising a fleet as America."
- "While we profess ourselves the subjects of Britain, we must, in the eye of foreign nations, be considered as rebels."

THINK ABOUT IT!

1. How might a pamphlet written by an Englishman mean something different to colonists than one written by a fellow colonist?
2. How did Thomas Paine's writing style help him gain popularity?

3. Why were the ideas in *Common Sense* so radical? Why might some people find them dangerous?
4. How did *Common Sense* affect the course of the American Revolution?

GLOSSARY

advocate: To argue for or support a cause or policy.

convert: A person who has changed from one way of thinking to another.

corset: A woman's close-fitting supporting undergarment that gets its rigidity from animal bones.

democracy: The free and equal right of every person to participate in a government.

Enlightenment: A movement in the 18th century marked by the rejection of traditional beliefs in favor of logic and science.

Founding Father: One of the leading figures in the founding of the United States.

grievance: A complaint.

hereditary: Passed from parent to child.

Parliament: The lawmaking body of England, now the United Kingdom.

Quaker: One who belongs to a particular faith that believes in equality for all people, strong families and communities, and peace.

radical: Having extreme political or social views that are not shared by most people.

succession: The order or right of taking a throne or title after someone else.

tyranny: Cruel and unfair treatment by people with power over others.

unconventional: Not in line with what is typically done.

FIND OUT MORE

Books

Fowler, Natalie. *A U.S. Independence Time Capsule: Artifacts of the Nation's Beginnings*. Mankato, MN: Capstone Press, 2020.

Miloszewski, Nathan. *Patriots and Loyalists*. New York, NY: PowerKids Press, 2020.

Websites

American Revolution
kids.britannica.com/kids/article/American-Revolution/353711
Explore the history behind the American Revolution.

Road to Revolution for Kids: 1776 Common Sense, Thomas Paine
revolution.mrdonn.org/commonsense.html
Read more about the important questions *Common Sense* raised for American colonists.

Thomas Paine
www.ducksters.com/history/american_revolution/thomas_paine.php
Learn more about Thomas Paine, the writer behind *Common Sense*.

INDEX